Scamp and Tramp

Guyla Nelson

and

Saundra Scovell Lamgo

Illustrated by David Grassnick

American Language Series
A Beginning Short Vowel Reader
with Consonant Clusters

Alpha Omega Publications
Chandler, Arizona

For all boys and girls
who wish to
become readers of
good books —
and especially the
Book of Books, the Bible

Stories

Shep and the Pups

Shep is a big, big dog.

Shep has six pups.

The pups nip at Shep in fun.

Nip, nip, nip.

The pups nap by Shep.

A Red Ship

Josh has a ship.

The ship is not big.

His ship is red.

Josh will dash to the tub.

He will set his red ship in the tub.

The Cat and the Cup

Wham! The cup fell.

When the cup fell, it hit the cat's leg.

The cat ran and hid.

The Big Bug

Whop! Whop! Whop!
Sam hit at the big bug.
Did Sam miss the bug?
Yes, Sam did miss it.

Whop! Whop! Whop!
Dad hit at the big bug.
Did Dad hit the bug?
Yes, Dad hit the big bug.

The Box of Nuts

Rob will get a box.

He will fill it with nuts.

Then he will shut the lid.

Rob will run with the box.

He will go to the man in the shop.

Will he sell the nuts?

Yes, Rob will sell them to the man.

Bob and His Pup

Bob will munch on a bag of chips.

Then he will fill his mug with punch.

Bob's pup is with him.

The pup will munch on his lunch.

The pup will not munch on chips.

He will munch on a pup's lunch.

The lunch will fill Bob and the pup.

The Buns

Bev will fix buns.

The buns will be hot.

She will set the buns on the bench.

Then Bev and Mom will go to lunch.

The Lads and the Hens

The lads will shell the nubs.

That will be a big job, but it will be fun.

Can we tell why the lads had to shell the nubs?

The hens had to be fed.

The hens ran to the lads to get lunch.

The lads had fun.

The hens had fun.

Lunch

Mom got a big ham at the shop.

She set the ham in a pan.

She put a lid on top of the pan.

She let the ham get hot in the pan.

Then Sis put the ham on the buns.

Mom set the chips by the buns.

Ned will sit by Sis at lunch.

Dad will sit by Mom.

Chop the Logs

Ted will whizz up the path.

Then Chad will whizz up the path.

The lads will run to the shed.

Dad is by the shed.

Ted will go to the shed to get his ax.

Chad will get an ax.

Dad will let them chop logs with him.

Chop, chop, chop.

Chad will chop logs.

He will chop the logs with his ax.

His ax is not dull.

Chop, chop, chop.

Dad will chop logs.

Ted will cut lots of logs.

Then Chad, Ted, and Dad will put the logs in the shed.

Tish

Tish will rush to the box.

She will get a doll.

She will get a sash.

She will fix the sash on the doll.

What fun that will be!

The Dutch Lad and Lass

Jan will sketch with a pen.

She will sketch a Dutch lad.

Then she will sketch a Dutch lass.

The Dutch lad has a tan hat.

The Dutch lass has a pink sash.

Up the Hill

Chet runs up the hill.

Dad thinks that he and Ching can catch up with Chet.

19

Dad and Ching run and run.

Chet runs.

Up, up, up run Chet and Dad and Ching.

Will Dad and Ching catch Chet?

Yes, Dad and the dog will catch Chet at
the top of the hill.

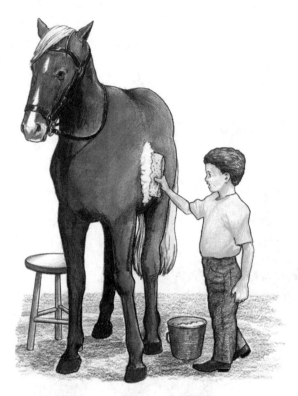

Seth and Patch

Patch is a mess.

Patch will get a bath.

He will get wet.

Seth will rub lots of suds on Patch.

The suds will get the mud off.

Then Seth and Patch will go up the path to the shed.

Patch will get his lunch in the shed.

The Tank

Bang, bang, bang!

Jeff has a bat.

He hits the bat on the tank.

Bang, bang, bang!

Chip tells Jeff not to bang on the tank.

The tank is big.

The tank is tan.

The Songs

Ross will sing a song.

Ken will sing a song.

Then Ron will sing a song.

Ron's song is long.

His song is a fun song.

Ron has fun as he sings to Ross and Ken.

The Bell

Thad hung his bag on the peg.

Bang! The bag fell off the peg!

The bag fell in the fish tank.

A bell was in the bag.

The bell fell in the fish tank.

The bell got wet.

Did the bell ring when it was wet?

No, the bell did not ring in the fish tank.

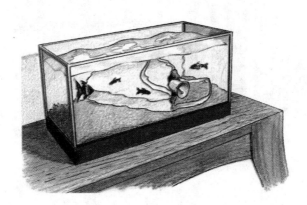

Nan's Bank

Nan has a bank.

The bank is big.

The bank is pink.

Nan's big pink bank is a pig.

The bank sits on the bench by Nan's bed.

Nan will put cash in the bank.

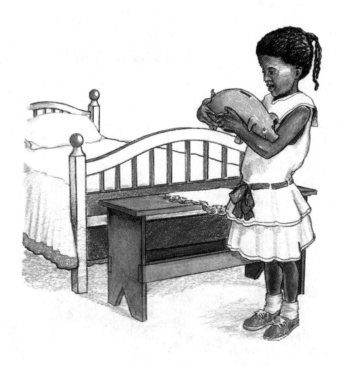

Sing and Sing

Let us thank God and sing.

Let us sing and sing.

We will sing of God.

We will sing and be glad.

Let us thank God and sing.

The Pink Shell

Beth has a shell.

The shell is pink.

The shell is thin.

Beth will rush to Dan with the shell.

Can Dan tell Beth what was in this shell?

The Mink

The mink ran to the bush and hid.

The mink hid as the pup ran by.

A pup ran by the bush.

The mink was glad that the pup did
not catch him.

The Dish in the Hutch

Ann has a dish.
The dish is pink.
Ann will put a lid
on the pink dish.

Can Ann set the dish in the hutch?

The hutch has a latch on it.

Ann will get on the bench with the dish.

She will push the latch.

Then she will set the dish in the hutch.

She will get off the bench.

The pink dish with the lid will be in the hutch.

34

The Red Jet

Jim has a red jet.

He will let his pal, Max, fly the jet.

The jet will go up and up.

What fun it is to fly the red jet!

Sing a Song

Miss Hill will let us sing.

Sing a song with us.

We will sing of God.

We will be glad as we sing.

Tim and the Sled

Tim fell off the sled.
He cut his leg.

Dad will fix Tim's leg.

Dad will put Tim on the sled.

Dad and Tim will go up the hill to the van.

Dad will set Tim in the van.

Then Dad will put the sled in the van.

Sid

Sid has a red cup and a bag of chips.

He will sit on the rug with his cup
and chips.

Sid will munch on his chips and sip
his punch.

Al

Al can wink.

He winks at Mom.

He winks at Dad.

Al winks at Sis.

He will wink at his dog.

He will wink at his fish.

Will Al wink as he naps?

Mel

Todd can wink.
Pat can wink.
Rich can wink.

Can Mel wink? No.

He cannot wink.

Mel thinks and thinks, but he cannot wink.

The Top

Rex will spin the red top.

He will watch it spin and spin.

Rex claps as the top spins.

What fun it is to spin the red top!

The Flax

Liz will put the flax on the bank.

Then she will let the flax dry.

When the flax is dry, Liz will spin with it.

Then she will cut a dress from the cloth.

Deb

Splash, splash.

Slosh, slosh.

Did Deb step in the mud and slush?

Yes, she did.

Deb got mud and slush on the pink dress.

She got a spot on the hat.

Deb is a mess.

The Stag

Watch the stag by the spring!
He will get a drink from the spring.

The stag gets his drink.
Then he slips off into the grass.

Tom and Jen

Tom will go on the bus.

Jen will go with Tom on the bus.

She thinks it is fun to be on the bus with lots of pals.

The bus will stop.

Jen will get off the bus.

Tom will get off the bus.

Jen and Tom will go to Miss Bell's class.

What will Tom and Jen do?

Jen and Tom will sit still in class.

Miss Bell will tell them of God.

Class will be lots of fun.

The Cat

The cat will scratch and scratch at the bench.

Mom will be cross.

What can she do to stop this?

Mom will bring in a log.

She will set it by the cat.

Then the cat can scratch and scratch on the log and not on the bench.

Frank

Frank will get a drink.

He will fill the glass and drink from it.

Then he will set his glass in the sink.

Frank will run to the swing.

He will swing with his pal, Greg.

What fun that will be!

The Thrush

The thrush sits on a branch.

He will try to get a bug from the branch.

What will he do then?

Then the thrush will sit on the branch and sing.

His song will not be shrill.

It will not be a sad song.

He will sing a glad song as he sits on the branch.

Ed's Drum

Ed has no drum.

He will fix a drum from a tin can.

Thump, thump, thump will go the drum.

Ed has fun as he taps on his drum.

King and the Ham

The shank of ham hangs in the shed.

King, the dog, jumps at the ham.

Watch him! Will he grab the ham?

Dad runs to the shed.

Dad will catch King.

He will tell King, "No!"

King runs from the shed.

King did not get the ham.

The Glass Lamp

Wham! The glass lamp fell!

Did the glass lamp smash as it hit the bench?

Yes, it did!

Mom will be sad.

She was fond of the glass lamp.

Scamp and Tramp

Scamp is Tramp's chum.

Scamp runs and jumps.

Tramp romps and romps.

Scamp will tag Tramp.

Tramp is Scamp's chum.

The Box

Hank will send a box to his pal.
What is in the box?

The box has a pen in it.

The pen is not long.

Hank's pal will be glad to get the pen.

At the Pond

Pam, Kit, and Nell swam in the pond.
Watch Pam splash as she swims!

Then Pam and Kit sat on a raft.
Did Nell splash them?

Yes, she did splash them.
Nell, Pam, and Kit had fun at the pond.

The Wind and the Dish

The wind is brisk.

Will the wind hit the dish?

Peg thinks it will.

Whish! The wind hit the dish.

Wham! The dish fell!

What a crash!

Dad cannot fix the dish.

Peg will toss the bits of the dish in the trash.

The Frog

The frog sits and sits on the stump.

The stump is at the edge of the pond.

The frog sits still.

He will not hop.

The frog snaps at a big fly.
Did he catch the fly?
Yes, the frog got the fly.

Cliff and Fred

Cliff is in the crib.

He is not a big lad yet.

He will nap in his crib.

Cliff will fuss and cry when he wants to get up.

Fred will go to get Mom.

Mom will get Cliff from the crib.

Then Cliff and Fred will romp and romp on the rug.

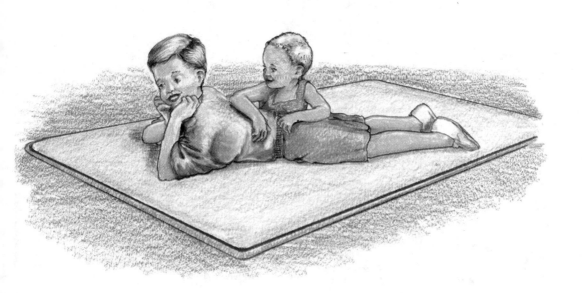

The Trip

Glen wants to go on a trip with Dad and Mom.

Glen thinks the trip will be fun.

What can Glen do in the van?

He can sit and he can stand in the van.

Glen can get a nap in the van.
Then he can stretch and stretch.

The Shag Rug

The shag rug is red.

Kim sits on the rug.

Kim thinks that the shag rug is soft.

A Trip to the Ranch

Russ went on a long trip.

He went on a jet.

He went to a big ranch.

Russ had fun.

He got to fish in a pond.

He slept on a bunk.

He got to chop logs.

Russ was sad when he had to go.

He went on a jet.

Drip, Drip, Drop

Drip, drip, drop.
The sand is wet.
Drip, drip, drop.
The grass is wet.

Drip, drip, drop.

Jill gets wet.

She runs to the shed.

Drip, drip, drop.

Drip, drip, drop.

The frog gets wet.

What fun it is to let the drops hit him!

He just sits and sits on his log.

He will not hop off.

The Bank

Dad wants to get cash.

We will go to the bank.

Dad has a bag with him.

The man at the desk hands the cash to Dad.

Then Dad puts the cash in his bag.

But what is this pink thing the man puts in my hand? What can it be?

This is a swell gift. Yum, yum!

We thank the man and then go from the bank.

The Wind

A blast of wind swept past me.
The strong wind hit my hat.
My hat fell off.

The gust of wind sent my hat into the dust.

Will the wind let me catch my hat?

Yes, but the hat has dust on it!

What a mess! Let me brush off the dust!

The wind had fun with my hat.

The Lost Plug

Clint is a grump.

He lost the plug.

He cannot jump in the tub till he gets a plug.

When he gets the plug, then he can sit
in the tub.

Clint will put his ship in the tub.

Clint's bath will be fun.

The Bluff

Lon ran up on the bluff.

Skip ran to the top of the bluff.

Madge will not run.

She will try to get to the top of the bluff as fast as she can.

From the top of the bluff, Lon and Skip can spot Madge.

At last she will get to the top.

Then Madge, Lon, and Skip will rest.

Kent

Kent sits at his desk.

He will try to do his best.

He will spell the best he can.

Then he will print the best he can.

Kent will do the best he can on his test.

Mom and Dad will be glad.
God will be glad.
Kent will be glad that he did his best.

A Big Bump

Jed ran fast.

Did he trip?

Yes, and he fell.

He has a big bump on his leg.

Jed has a cast on his leg.

He will not run and jump.

He must rest.

Jed will be glad when his leg gets well.

Then he will get the cast off his leg.

Then Jed will run and jump.

He will be glad.

A Cat and a Dog

The cat will sit on the ledge.

She will not budge when the dog runs up to the ledge.

She will just sit still.

At last the dog will go.

The cat will stretch on the ledge and nap in the sun.

Bron

Bron sits at the desk.

She plans what she will sketch.

She will sketch a clam.

Next she will sketch
a skunk.

Then she will sketch a shrimp.

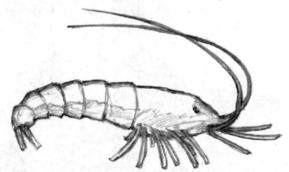

Bron can sketch well.

Bron has skill.

Bron's skill is a gift from God.

Meg

Meg is a doll.

She is a plump doll.

Meg sits on the shelf.

Meg cannot run.

She cannot jump.

She cannot swim.

Meg is just a doll.

Dad and Jud

Dad will cut the hedge.
He will let Jud help him.

    When the hedge is cut, then Dad will cut
the grass.
    Jud will trim the edge of the grass as
Dad cuts the grass.

Then Dad and Jud will rest next to the big shrub.

Dad will get a drink.

He will nudge Jud, and Jud will get a drink.

Gwen

Gwen has on Mom's wig.

She has on Mom's dress.

Next she puts Mom's hat on top of the wig.

Mom and Dad grin when Gwen steps
in front of them.

Gwen thinks it is fun to dress in
Mom's things.

The Lost Cap

What did Les do with his cap?

He thinks it is lost.

Mom sent him to try to find it.

Did Les get the cap?

Yes, the cap was in the dust next to the big elm.

My Flag

My flag is a grand old flag.
This flag is the flag of my land.

I will stand up tall as I watch my flag pass.
I will pledge to my flag as it flaps in
the wind.

Camp

Dad and Matt will go to a shop.

Dad will rent a tent.

He will rent a cot.

Then Dad and Matt will get in the red van.

Up, up, up the hill the van will go.

At dusk, Dad and Matt will stop and camp next to a cliff by a pond.

At camp it is crisp, brisk, and damp.

Dad will set up the tent.

Matt will chop logs.

Next Dad and Matt will rest on the bank of the pond and fish.

Fran Helps

Fran has a red dress.

She must not toss the dress on the bed.

Fran must hang the dress on a peg.

This will help Mom.

Fran runs to help Mom fix lunch.
Mom will fix yams and ham.
Fran will fix buns and jam.
She will get milk to drink.

Sin

God is sad when we sin.

He must judge all sin.

We must ask God to help us.

He will be glad when we ask Him to help us be kind and do right.

Bill and Brent

Dad went in to shop.

Bill did not go in.

He sat in the van.

Bill spots Brent.

Brent is Bill's chum.

Honk, honk went the van.

Brent spots Bill.

He runs to the van.

He jumps in the van with Bill.

The lads sit and sing.

Then Bill tells Brent of the dog his dad got him last month.

Brent tells Bill of the fence he and his dad will fix.

At last Bill's dad gets to the van.
Then Brent jumps from the van.
Dad and Bill must go.

Fudge

Sis will fix a pan of fudge.

Dot will help.

She will set the pan of fudge on the ledge.

When Dan gets up from his nap, Dot
will cut the fudge.

She will hand a wedge of fudge to Dan.

He will smack his lips. Yum, Yum!

The Lodge

We will go on a trip in a van.

We will go to a big lodge.

The trip will be lots of fun.

Dad will go with Rick and me to the
pond to fish.

Rick will sit on the bank next to me.

We will try to catch lots of fish.

Mom will sit on the edge of the pond
and mend socks.

We will snack on a lunch as we sit on
the grass.

Then we will go back to the lodge to rest.

The Shock

Gus has wet hands.

No! No! Gus.

Do not put the plug in!

Gus will get a shock.

Gus will run to Dad.

Dad will hug him.

He will tell Gus not to plug things in with wet hands.

Tubs, the Cub

Tubs is a cub.

He is not big yet.

He runs and romps.

Then he rests on the rock.

Next Tubs gets fish from the pond.

Tubs will munch on his lunch.

A Sack of Tacks

Jack had a big sack of tacks.

He set the sack on the bench.

The sack fell off the bench.

Did Jack kick the sack? Yes.

Jack had to pick up the tacks that fell.

Chuck and His Duck

Chuck has a pet duck.

The duck is black.

The duck is in a pen by the shed.

Chuck sits on a rock by the pen.

He pets his duck.

The duck is Chuck's pal.

The Red Truck

Don's dad has a red truck.

His red truck will go fast up the hill.

Don is in the truck.

Grant is in the truck.

Spot is in the back of the truck.

He sits still.

Vince

Vince drinks from a cup.

He spills on his pants.

What a mess he is!

Vince must get help.

He runs to his mom.

She will help him.

Chip and Zip

Chip is tan.

Zip is tan.

Zip is Chip's twin.

Chip runs fast.

He gets on a branch.

Chip hid from his twin.

Zip cannot find Chip.

Scott

Swish, swish.
Scott will
brush the
grass off
the path.

Then he will stack the grass next to the trash can.

He will stack the twigs and a big branch next to the trash can.

Scott is a big help to Dad.

The Duck and the Fish

The duck will dunk to try to catch the fish.
Did he catch the fish?

Yes, he did.

The fish was not big.

The fish was not long.

But the duck had a lunch of fish.

Brad and His Ax

Brad has a red and black ax.

He will cut sticks with his ax.

He will put a bunch of sticks on the bench.

Then he will split logs with his ax.

He will stack the logs.

The Skunk

The skunk is on the rock.

He is black but has a strip on his back that is not black.

We must not stand by the skunk.

We must not pet him.

He smells bad.

We will be glad if the skunk will go on
past us.

Bess and Jess

Bess has a big bag.

She has jacks and a doll in the bag.

Jess has a bag.

His bag has a strap on it.

Jess has a drum and a bell in his bag.

Jess can put his bag on his back.

Puff and Muff

Puff is a chick.

Muff is a chick.

Puff is soft.

Puff has fluff.

Muff is soft.

Muff has fluff.

Puff will rest.

Muff will run and jump.

The Pink Dress

Trish can pin a hem.

She will stick pins in the dress.

She will fix the silk dress.

The dress is pink.

The dress is soft.

Trish will be glad when she has the hem in the dress.

Then she will press the pink dress.

A Rip

Dick's pant leg has a rip in it.

Dick will get a pin and try to fix the rip.

No, no.

Dick cannot fix the rip.

Who can help him?

Dick will go to Mom.

He will watch as she mends the rip.

Then he will thank Mom.

The Fox

The fox is sly.

He hid by the rock.

Will he try to get the hen and chicks?

The hen and chicks must run.
Can Brett hit the fox?
He gets a stick.

The fox runs fast.
Brett will not let the fox get the hen and the chicks.

Dell's Clock

Tick, tock.

Tick, tock.

Dell's clock ticks as it sits on the shelf.

The clock struck six.

The clock tells Dell when to get up.

She must put on a pink frock.

Dell must help Mom.

Then she will rush to class.

The Duck

This is a big duck.

She is soft.

She has a bell.

The duck can swim.

She dips in the pond.

She can go splash, splash.

Then she gets up on the grass.
She must rest.

She swims fast.
When she swims, the bell rings.
The bell ding, dings.
The duck can go quack, quack.

The Black Gnat

The black gnat is not big, but she can fly fast.

She will fly to the ledge and land on a bun.

The gnat will not lunch on the bun.

She will fly from the ledge and will land in the grass.

The Knot

Lance got a knot in the string.

He will try to get the knot from the string.

Can he do it?

No, he must cut the knot from the string.

The Gifts

Mom can knit.

She will knit socks.

The socks will be a gift to Nat.

She will knit a hat.

The hat will be a gift to Von.

Did the socks fit Nat?

Yes, the socks fit Nat.

Did the hat fit Von?

Yes, the hat fit Von.

Stan's Pet

Stan has a pet.

The pet is not big.

The pet can sit on Stan's thumb.

He will get crumbs from Stan's hand.

Then he will sing and sing.

Can we think of this pet?

The Soft Lamb

Ben has a pet lamb.

The lamb is soft.

The lamb licks Ben's wrist.

The lamb and Ben will romp in the grass.

Then the lamb will munch on the grass in Ben's hand.

The lamb is a pal to Ben.

The Wren

The wren will fix a nest.

She will sit and sit on the nest.

When it is hot, she still sits on the nest.

When it gets cold, she still sits on the nest.

When the wind hits the wren, she still sits on the nest.

Can we tell why?

She has six eggs in the nest.

She will sit on them till the eggs hatch.

The Wreck

Kev and Mack will run to the sand.

Kev has a van in his hand.

Mack has a bus.

Kev will dig a path in the sand.

He will run his van on the path.

Then Mack will run his bus on the path.

Bang! The bus and the van had a wreck.

Kev will get his big truck.

He will run his truck on the path to the wreck.

The truck will help get the bus and the van back to the shop.

The Phlox

Val cut the pink and red phlox.

Val has the phlox in a tall glass.

She will set the glass on the sill.

The Path

The bricks sit by the bench.

Dad will fix a path with the bricks.

The path will go to the back of the shop.

Then the brick path will go past the shed
to the pond.

Mom will plant phlox by the path at the edge of the pond.

Phil will rest by the pond and smell the phlox.

Quince Jam

Mom has a sack of quince.

Steph will help Mom.

Steph will cut up the quince.

Then Mom will fix jam from the quince.

Steph thinks the quince jam will go well on hot buns.

A Thick Quilt

Von has a thick red quilt.

She will put the quilt on the bed.

The soft quilt is a gift from Von's mom and dad.

Von is so glad that the red quilt will be on the bed. She tells them, "Thanks, Mom and Dad."

The Man

The man will be a help to God.

He has a quill in his hand.

The quill is a pen.

He will dip the quill in the ink.

Then the man will print with the quill.

He will print on skin.

Then he will put the skin on the ledge
to let it dry.

When the skin is dry, the man will roll up the skin.

He will set it in a big pot.

The man is a big help to God.

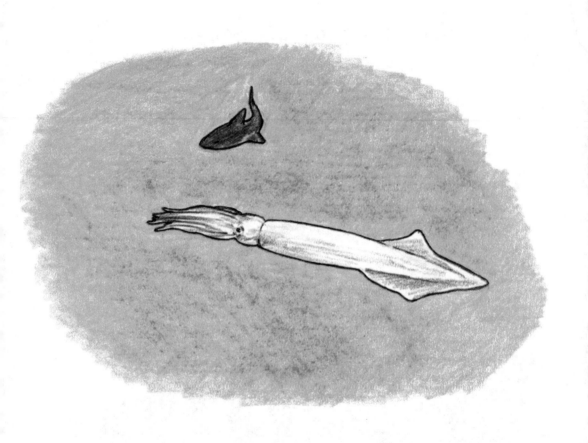

A Squid

The squid swims and swims.

He swims fast.

A big fish will try to catch the squid.

175

Did the fish catch the squid?

No, the squid was quick.

He swam so fast that the big fish did not catch him.